IT'S JUST A GAME…

MY ASS

Dad's *Youth Sports* Playbook

By

Tom Piper

Published by September Moon Publishing™

With love to Lori, Alex & Zach

Gonna miss it

Table of Contents

Pre-Game

Youth sports have been around since the time of the ancient Assyrians, who enjoyed log rolling on top of children before they discovered logs. But the halcyon days of farm boys scraping together a game of sand lot football or baseball and then going on to star at their high school and ultimately Notre Dame has been replaced by a far more complicated, and crushingly expensive, reality.

Out of the women's rights movement (something we wholeheartedly support here!) came the notion that everyone (meaning girls) should play sports as the ultimate expression of equality by conquering that distinctly male world. And that sort of spilled over to everyone *else* (meaning boys who really wouldn't have been allowed anywhere near the ball field in the old days and are now actually *encouraged* to play).

Combine that with the Echo Boom parenting era, when all of the famously self-indulgent Boomers decided that their parents' approach to youth sports ("ride your damn bike to practice" and "I didn't know you were on the baseball team, son") was probably responsible for at least a portion of their dependence on Zoloft and Ambien. Thus, the opportunity to live vicariously through the exploits of their own, properly nurtured offspring proved irresistible.

Wrap all of this up in an explosion of popularity for sports in general and you have the recipe for the youth-sports-obsessed jungle that you are now entering into.

Yet you may still hear the refrain *It's Just a Game* from time to time. It's usually offered as some sort of patronizing verbal valium from someone who would rather watch a cooking show than a game 7.

You're not that guy. And it's definitely not just a game.

This book is your playbook for survival.

Chapter 1: Gaming Your Genetics

Getting Past First Base

Perhaps you are still unmarried, childless, and thus understandably in a state of blissful narcissism that makes preposterous the idea that you would ever care about anyone else's abs as much as your own. Or maybe, like my smug little brother in California, you still have tiny little children and you somehow imagine that sports will be a simple enrichment activity, not unlike trips to the zoo or *Baby Einstein* videos. I'm here to save you time and heartache.

Youth sports are not a choice for you. Your boys, or girls, will be gladiators in the nation's coliseum. So you need to seed the ground, as it were, with your seed. If you are not yet married, it is important that you pick a suitable mate to ensure your progenies their rightful place within the athletic pantheon. There are many ways to pick a bride, but it's important that you take the approach best suited to your particular situation.

Take this helpful test:

1. Are you white?
   a. Exceptionally __
   b. No __

2. Did you play varsity in any high school sport?
   a. Yes __
   b. No __

Answer **NO** if it was in golf at any high school north of the Mason Dixon line and east of California.

Answer **NO** if it was as a male member of the dance team.

Answer **NO** if you attended a small private school with names such as Crossroads or Friendship Commons or it was affiliated with the Quakers in any way. (Lovely people Quakers, lousy athletes).

3. Do you consider badminton a sport?
   a. Yes __
   b. No __

4. What is your immediate response when, while watching the Winter Olympics, ice dancing comes on?
   a. I hit record on the DVR __
   b. I watch for a bit and then see what else is on __
   c. I throw up in my mouth a little __

5. When new league teams form at the office for softball, hoops, or flag football, does the team captain make a special pilgrimage to your cubicle even before putting the flyer up in the break room?
   a. Yes __
   b. No __

6. Can you dunk?
   a. Yes __
   b. No __

If you answered Yes to the last question, proceed to Breeding **Plan A**. All others: **Plan B**.

Breeding Plan A:
Marry for love and/or looks and rely on those absurdly over-the-top athletic genes of yours to combine with the lovely lass of your choice to get both Johnny Damon's looks (her contribution) with Gretsky's hands. Couple, copulate, canoodle, and await the next Derek Jeter or Tom Brady.

Breeding Plan B:
Acknowledge that while you have, to your way of thinking at least, a "real feel for the game," your parents saddled you with a genetic golf bag that may leave you a few irons short of the green. Better to play "best ball" with the right woman. So, do not marry the one with the fantastic boobs if she failed to pass her primary school physical fitness test because she couldn't weave through six orange cones in the gym without going ass over tea kettle. Enjoy her boobs for a time (it would be a shame not to), but cut her loose before too long because you will only resent her later for failing to compensate for the fact that *you* were never able to break 8 seconds in the 50-yard dash.

Instead of great boobs, go with great ball control. Take your dates out and test them. Do they run like a girl? Dribble a basketball like it's a giant two-handed yo-yo? Or … can they rip a softball right past your ear on a rope?

Did she captain her high school lax team to a state title? Hell, even if she bowls decently, it may improve the genetic soup considerably, depending on if you're lying to me right now about whether you actually *do* bat cleanup for your company softball team.

Your Play:

The point here is if your sperm can't swim like Michael Phelps, then you need some eggs that have got a little game. Make it so.

If, however, the love train has already sailed and you're by this time blissfully saddled to a soul mate who runs *and* throws like a girl, well, fear not. I've still got some advice for you here on making lemonade with your chromosomal lemons.

Chapter 2: Spring Training

Teaching Your Toddler to hit Opposite Field

Congratulations Dad. You're now the proud daddy of a 2-something-year-old and the window of critical athletic development time is already closing. You do not have a moment to lose. The super-annoying guy at the end of the cul-de-sac with the BMW 7-Series already claims his 3-year-old can throw a serviceable curve ball. A ridiculous lie for certain, but it has you a little spooked all the same.

The Equipment Makes the Man

So here's what you're going to do Champ: Get off the sofa on Sunday morning, put on an old-but-still-fetching sweatshirt, and get to Target. You are now going to buy your way to vicarious glory. Get the big cart and start loading up the plastic bats, balls, hockey sticks, mini baseball gloves, lax sticks, soccer nets, pitch backs, tee-ball sets, tennis racquets, and John Daly Bubba Jr. golf sets. Trust me, Dad, this is the good part. This is all the awesome multi-colored swag you never had as a kid, in fact, did not even exist when you were a kid. China hadn't been invented yet. But now that it has, these treasures can all be had for seemingly laughable prices when compared to the hours of enjoyment it will bring when you're sitting in the stands at the College World Series and the ESPN camera pans to the proud parents shot (look excited and yet as though you always knew this was going to happen).

Take it all home, give your wife that look that says, *"Of course he needs all of this and I know it's not his birthday and please back off Baby Mama — athletic development is MY DEPARTMENT!"*

There will of course be no sex this week, but you will be pretty exhausted from playing with all the new toys anyway.

Progress is rapid at this age. You will be stunned at just how quickly the ball goes from smacking him in the face (15-minute time-out to run to mom in tears, get a chocolate chip cookie, and then be slowly coaxed back out to the yard for more instruction) to having him stabbing at it, to making glove-to-ball contact. At this rate, actual catching will surely come before Christmas, or at least the following one.

Your Play:

Buy fun swag.

Load it into the yard.

Drill your future superstar until he is so frustrated and upset that you both get a free pass to watch sports on TV for the rest of the afternoon while eating nachos your wife made.

Chapter 3: Rec League

Let the Games Begin

Rec, church league, YMCA, or some other community organization will be your first foray into organized sports. The following are the important facts about your early Rec days:

Fact #1 It's Cheap

That first tab for youth soccer with a volunteer coach will cost you roughly $30 for "the season," which consists of a handful of practices and games. This is of course a huge bait and switch, as you will soon be spending the better part of your income and hoped for retirement funds on youth sports until they are 18, at which point you will spend whatever is left on college.[1] So enjoy these early value days.

Fact #2 It's Cute (sort of)

There are lots of moms (some cute) and dads and adorable little kids running around. There is laughing, shouting, screaming, giggling, and crying. And there are lots and lots of video cameras and phones recording it all. There is usually no official score kept, but every dad on

---

[1] Yes, you're way ahead of me here, but the athletic scholarship should be only considered *probable* and not definite at this point.

the pitch or in the gym is of course keeping his own private, and likely inaccurate, count.

Fact #3 It's Coed

Thanks to Women's Lib, Title IX, the sexual revolution, and Billie Jean King, it was decided that girls and boys should play their games together.[2] Mercifully, this ends fairly soon after the first few rec teams, but it must be suffered through at first. I remember my son Zach's first basketball team, where we had four boys and three girls. These girls simply wanted to work on cheers and had to be forced onto the court. They regarded the basketball as some offensive spherical object that they were required to touch from time to time. Meanwhile, the boys were like golden retrievers presented with a tennis ball — unbridled enthusiasm.

Now of course you're asking, *"What about the girls who were total jocks in high school? Weren't they little tomboys?"* I'm sure that they were, it's just that none of them were on my son's basketball team.

Fact #4 It's About the Snacks
Most kids at this age hate being dragged to sports and will be gone just as soon as they can develop a serviceable right jab to take mom with. So the only way to get them out there even at this early stage is with a

---

[2] I was in middle school when coed PE first swept the nation. We were playing flag football with all the really cute girls in the eighth grade when Jim King went to rip off my flag, but instead managed to rip my gym shorts clean off. I've not even come close to recovering from that moment.

healthy bribe following every game and practice. But when I say healthy, I mean only in the sense that it is substantial. Most of these kids already look like Augustus Gloop, which is why their parents probably think they should turn out for rec soccer to begin with. And yet, maybe because nothing says "*I love you*" like a Little Debbie snack cake — 200 calories of soccer practice is met with 1,200 calories of love.

A "snack schedule" will be put together by one of the moms and pushed out by email to all, instructing you which day you are required to bring "sports" drinks, candy bars, cookies, chips, "fruit" rollups, and a vast array of garbage in reward for the kids' big effort that day. You cannot fight the moms on this. If you try to suggest something healthy like orange slices, they will dismiss you with a look that suggests you also must hate puppies. So just steal and enjoy as many of the Ding Dongs as you can to try to protect as much of your kid's cardiovascular system as possible. They might need it later.

Fact #5 It's Everyone
The great weeding out has not begun. There is no meritocracy here. Trophies for all! Seventy-five percent of all kids who start with sports at this age will determine at a fairly young age that they hate sports, suck at them, would vastly prefer to be in modern dance or band, watching TV, playing XBOX, studying cell division in mollusks, or just eating toaster pastries. They will inform their parents of their loathing for sports once they develop a sufficient vocabulary. But for now you're stuck with them on your future child prodigy's team and it will

drive you crazy. You will tell yourself, *"Hey, they're just kids. What does it matter as long as everyone is having fun, right?"* But it *does* matter. I promise you, Dad, you will very quickly also want to **win** these games, no matter how meaningless they might be.

This is how the conversation in your head will go:

*"This is great, just absolutely terrific! It's a beautiful Saturday morning, we're outside, the family is together. I've got a Grande Non-Fat Latte from $tarbucks in my hand and I'm sitting in our new fold-up camp chairs from Target that are surprisingly comfortable and have this great little pocket for my coffee. The kids seem to be having fun and it is all good! It really is. Love this ... really, just great .... **That said**, and maybe this is just the caffeine talking, but I mean, hey, as long as we're out here, we might as well **try** to win, right? I mean, seriously, I don't care at all, but somebody has to win right? And with just a little effort ... if the coach would just tell No. 3 to freaking pass the ball once in a while, that would help, and for Christ's sake, No. 26 just stands there! I mean I know you have to play her, but she is clearly miserable. Do her and **us** a favor and let her stand on the sidelines instead of on the field and she'll thank you! And that fat little kid with three left feet, holy Christ, if he kicks the ball out of bounds again instead of passing it to my son, who was wide open in front of the net, I am going to ring his chubby little neck!"*

After a while these little thought bubbles that were just in your head begin to emerge in the form of groans, polite profanities, and full-blown declaratives. And your wife will finally freeze you with a look that says "one more word and you're painting the deck all afternoon" while

17

making a mental note to skip the Starbucks stop next
weekend.

Fact #6 It's Equal Playing Time
Well of course it is, you say, "That's only fair." Everyone
paid the same amount of money. Everyone is out here to
get better. *Blah, blah, blah.* But you also realize that you
don't look forward to these little contests because you
enjoy watching the *team.* You look forward to them
because you like watching your kid. It is *that* simple. So
you do rather resent watching your guy coming off the
field *again* so that Mortimer Stumblebum can go back in.
And of course it *isn't* equal playing time. The coach's kid
and the coach's kid's best friend get a hell of a lot more
time than yours does. Nobody keeps a stop watch on it,
so it's all a judgment call and it's pretty damn obvious
that you're getting the short end of the stick, as it were.
You would like to mention this to the coach, but then you
start thinking, *what if he takes offense at my whining and
takes it out on my kid with even less PT?*

Fact #7 Coaches: You Get What You Paid For
Most coaches, at this stage, are doing this for one of two
reasons:

1. They have some time and a good heart. These
   guys are also frequently a few innings short of a
   complete game (which may explain all the time
   they have on their hands and the fact that they
   have remained positive and cheerful throughout
   life). These are the *Losers.*

2. They want to get more playing time for their kid and they ~~want~~ *intend* to win. These are the *Winners*.

Loser Coaches: Losing with a smile is still losing
They will make up four out of every five coaches you have at this level. In addition to being initially grateful that this guy is willing to put in all the hours, your first reaction to them will be, "He seems really nice and I think little Billy really likes him." And little Billy will continue to like him because he never makes them do hard drills (or any drills) and he never actually tries to command their attention long enough to teach them anything. You will generally lose all of your games with these coaches. That doesn't even seem possible given the ratio I gave you above about them being four out of every five coaches, and yet, math aside, your Loser coach will somehow manage to be just a bit worse than the other Loser coaches.

Winner Coaches: Winning ugly
These guys are already on their way. They have the whole thing from age 6 to a D1 scholarship mapped out in their heads while you're still trying to figure out which fields the YMCA meets at. They are three steps ahead of you before you've even started. You may tell yourself, *"Well the kids are 6, so it can't possibly matter yet."* But you're more than a little worried that it does. With luck, you may be on this team rather than any of the others that are coached by the Losers. If you are on the Winner's team, you will win every game because he has found a way to stack his team with the talent he has already somehow scouted. And winning is much more fun than you're quite ready to admit at this point.

Fact #8 Injuries Are Endemic

Injuries at this tender age are rife. Or to be more precise, drama is rife. In all my years of watching hundreds of rec league games, I never saw anyone who was *actually* injured. I *did* see soccer players go down with enough melodrama to make an Italian fútboler blush.

I saw hockey players who would lie on the ice for up to five minutes if they thought they had the crowd's rapt attention, even though they could no longer remember what exactly hurt. The kids at this age really crave the attention they can get from a wound suffered in battle. With hockey, all the players were required to "take a knee" in a gesture of respect and concern while the injured warrior was ministered to. Talk about gratifying. These kids would lie there until the coach had slithered all the way across the ice from the bench to the scene of the crime. Then they would breathlessly groan their answers to the coach's questions about where it hurt until it was abundantly clear that nothing was hurt or broken enough for them to continue the performance. The audience would clap as they were helped back to the bench. The kid was typically back on the ice by their next shift (two or three minutes), miraculously healed.

Some of the parents are even better. We were once watching a Little League game where the kid was hit by a grounder rather than fielding it and he crumpled to the ground in apparent agony. Protocol in these situations is for the ump to go to the player first and assess the damage before gesturing the coach over and before finally calling in the big guns, which of course are never necessary. That's the drill. This kid's parents, both heavy set and in their matching polo shirts, thundered around the fence and onto the diamond to their firstborn's side before the ump could even amble over from second base. Turns out their son had just been hit by a grounder.

In another case, while watching a 10-year-old game of hockey, one of our team parents had to be restrained from attacking the refs, so outraged was he by the sight of his son laid out on the ice. How he could be persuaded that it was the other kid's fault when his son was not only the world's biggest injury drama queen but also a downright nasty player himself, is a question only a biologist can properly answer. Once again, the kid never missed any shifts, despite taking "dirty" hits that would, evidently, put an NHL player out for a month.

Your Play:

Do not make the mistake of treating the rec years as the pre-season. The game is already **on**, even if you don't know it yet. Begin your campaign for ascendency within the social sports hierarchy that is already forming all around you.

e.g. Forge a friendship between the coach's kid and your own with play dates, over the top birthday presents, and false praise, even if your son or daughter can't stand them. Playing time is playing time.

And steal the good snacks. Your arteries are no longer the issue.

Chapter 4: Games People Play

Which Sport Should You Steer Jr. Toward?

An excellent question that I'm glad you asked. Here is the definitive guide to games you may be tempted to push your little superstar into.

Baseball & Softball – Still a Classic

Still the most American of all sports, and Little League is a must, provided the kid can make the all-star team (too many weak links on a regular-season team). Twelve talented little 12-year-old boys are perfectly sized for the small diamond. The combination is a really fun, exciting, engaging game of baseball, even without beer, which it turns out, is frowned upon at this level. Who knew? I attempted to explain that I had just never tried to watch baseball sober before, so I wasn't even sure how you do that.

There is more politics and back-room dealing on a Little League all-star team than at the Iowa Straw Poll, but it's worth it if you can get there. With a little luck, you might even get to states or regionals.

Then once that is done, switch to lacrosse. Youth baseball on the big field is a kind of fan torture. If you've ever been to a major league game that was sort of slow, with a handful of hits, no home runs, and ended in a lopsided 3-

to-0 score, well that's like a Roman orgy compared to a bunch of 13-year-olds trying to play the same game. Time to move on.

Basketball – Harder Than It Looks

Little hands and minds are not yet ready for this game when the first leagues begin to form around second and third grade. It may not seem like it at first, but there is a subtlety to the teamwork, footwork, and ball handling of basketball that utterly eludes your average 7-year-old. In fact, it pretty much eludes them until college, as far as I can tell.[3] If you ever want to remind yourself about the truth of Darwinism and the fact that we're only marginally evolved past your average anthropoid, just try to teach a group of sixth-graders the pick-and-roll without killing yourself, and them.

I'm just giving you fair warning. It's still a great high school sport and you've got to get your guy out there sooner than later of course if you want him to have a shot at that. Just be ready for some frustration and rather low scoring contests until middle school. And for God's sake, if your guy or gal is going to play hoops, teach them to go left. There is nothing worse than a one-handed dribbler.

---

[3] The great exception being of course the Mercer Island High School Islanders teams of '80-'81 and '81-'82. And *screw you,* Shadle Park. You lost!

Ice Hockey – The Sport of Kings

Ice is a relatively frictionless surface. Ice skates allow you to accelerate and travel over it at super-human speeds. And, unlike running, you can turn or stop on a dime because you have sharp blades on your feet. Thus, playing hockey is like having superpowers, like Mr. Incredible. And it's completely awesome.

Also, unlike basketball, it's reasonably enjoyable to watch the little guys play this game even before they have any real skills. And if your little Gretsky gets the hang of skating faster than the other little pylons, you'll really be in for a treat because he will basically score at will for a few seasons until the others catch on. If they can get near the net, they can score. This isn't like the NHL, where goalies are huge, padded like the Incredible Hulk, and have cat-like reflexes. The goalies in youth hockey couldn't stop a beach ball if it was slowly rolling toward the net, so scoring is higher than in youth basketball at times. And worst case, there are nearly constant on-ice collisions and Three Stooges-like physical comedy on display that will keep you richly entertained.

Lacrosse – Turf Hockey

Just like hockey (awesome) except played on grass which is generally easier to find than ice.

It's already old hat and very competitive in the traditional hot-bed states of Maryland, Virginia, and most of New England where "Lax Bros" reign supreme in the social pecking order. But if you are in the Midwest or the West, this could be your ticket to local glory, or at least give you a conversation starter at neighborhood barbecues. *"Now, what's the sport with sticks your lad plays again?"*

Football – Ow

I played for one year. My memories are of really boring practices with a lot of standing around interrupted by running some plays in which I think I was injured in some fashion on every single one, even when I wasn't on the field. This *is* a fun sport to watch on television (I'm told that the NFL is a very popular professional league), but actually playing it, not so much. And unless you live in Texas or Ohio, I don't think the girls really care who plays football anymore. So that motivation is gone.

But if you choose to ignore this advice, then I recommend defense. It seems a bit safer since you're doing the hitting. And I would surmise that a blindside sack of the quarterback, or grabbing a Pick 6, might actually rival sex for good clean fun.

Soccer – The Great Dumping Ground

I have no idea why the Brits invented a game of simulated warfare where you can't use the most useful part of your already fairly limited anatomy, but they did, and then spread it around The Empire before retreating to their present state as a largely irrelevant sporting nation. So we're stuck with it. Basically, everyone *can* play soccer, and so everyone does. It's where the vast majority of those who will never play another sport spend their short and disappointing careers before moving on to science club or dressing up Goth.

Soccer is also funny because, as Americans, it just seems we cannot figure this game out. I mean, kudos to the Women's World Cup Team and even to the men who have begun to make some respectable showings, but if you take your typical youth team, a bunch of 7-year-olds from any other country could beat the crap out of our 15-year-olds. They seem to get it in the water over there. I remember, when I was about 10, one of my youth soccer coaches was excited because there was some South American dude playing soccer for the university who had volunteered to come and help coach us. I will never forget this poor guy's frustration. He just couldn't believe we were so bad. I don't think he had ever seen a group of kids from his country, including toddlers, who so fundamentally didn't get the nature of the game and, worse, didn't seem to particularly care. He lasted one practice and we cheerfully went back to our distinctly American style of futbol, which consisted of running around wildly kicking and attacking in every direction.

Swimming & Wrestling – Extreme Character Building

No glory here. No girls or big crowds (no crowds at all usually). Just long miserable hours in a pool or a sauna-like torture chamber being beaten up by your betters. This is only for the masochists at heart. But there are good bonding opportunities in these crucibles of perdition. Both are dull as dirt to watch if you don't know the participants, but I will tell you from experience, if Jr. *is* out there, and you know all the competitors, you will find yourself yelling your head off with excitement in both cases. Strange, but true. Another cool thing about wrestling is that if you participate for even a single season — as I did before quitting because I could no longer bear the thought of spending every afternoon in a stuffy room full of mats and male bodies all glistening with sweat and suffering in ways I never before thought possible — then you will possess a strange and mysterious skill that will allow you to defeat in wrestling virtually anyone else who has not been taught the dark arts. If joined in battle, just stay out of upper-cut range and wrap up the legs, then unleash hell.

Cross Country & Track – The Sleeper

Not as horrible as swimming or wrestling, but still an all-guts-and-no-glory sport. Oregon probably isn't going to call, but D3 running is not out of the question if you've got any kind of game, since the competition for spots in a sport with absolutely no professional future isn't quite so ridiculous (even lacrosse has a pro league). This is also a good one for those of you whose kid has thus far failed to show any aptitude for any other sport whatsoever. VO2 Max is a peculiar thing, and the majority of great runners I have ever known were not good at other sports. They seem to come out of nowhere, or band. Frequently scrawny, often accompanied by irritating or plainly odd personalities; but they can run like the wind. Some of them even have that curious Prefontaine-like capacity for pain that truly separates the merely talented from the otherworldly.

Tennis – Andre Agony

The sport of my youth, so I'm biased against it. My experience with tennis was very similar to the one Andre Agassi eloquently details in his book, *Open*, only without the talent or the winning part. Otherwise, the book gives a pretty accurate portrayal of my life with the fuzzy yellow ball. I don't know why, but it's sort of a grind of a sport. Hit the ball, hit the ball, hit the ball, and repeat. And there's way too much time to *think* during a match ….

Think about how if you don't win this point, you may have dug yourself a hole that is too deep to get out of. Think about how good girls' No. 3, Michelle Moxley, looks in a tennis dress.

Think about how ...

"It's so freaking hot out. God, I hate playing at noon. My grip isn't really that good with all the sweat and, oh crap, I feel a major sweat bead building on my forehead and preparing to drop into my eyeball, temporarily blinding me, just as he serves his killer first serve, which always jams my backhand, unless he's thinking about going forehand side ... am I cheating too far left? Shit, do I have enough time to wipe that sweat off my brow? Has he already bounced the ball twice or was that the first one? Better, go for it and ... AAAGGGH. Crap."

So I may not be in a position to advise you on this one. Just go with your gut. (Get it? That was a pun for those of you old enough to know that tennis strings were once made with ... oh never mind).

Golf – Winston C. Said it Best

"Golf is a game whose aim is to hit a very small ball into an even smaller hole, with weapons singularly ill-designed for the purpose."- Winston Churchill

Not a real sport, just a *game*, like bowling, billiards or beer drinking. And it's super boring to watch, unless it is Sunday at the Masters and you're watching it on your 52-inch flat screen with a beer. But if you have to watch

29

your high school kid play a tournament on a soggy April day, without beer … And boys, do not let Tiger's sex life mislead you. Golf is not a babe magnet game. Money is a babe magnet game.

Your Play:

Hockey: because it's awesome. Or, one of the other ones.

Chapter 5: Coaches

Where Have You Gone, Joe ~~DiMaggio~~ Paterno?

Our Coaching Fantasy

We have all been raised with the John Wooden, Vince
Lombardi, and Coach K coaching ideals. These gods of
men have it all: brains, strategy, discipline, tough love,
and a deft, almost uncanny, ability to get the most out of
the crazy quilt of characters that make up their teams over
the years. These guys are winners. They are inspiring and
we worship them. As a result, we think that the men and
women who go into the hobby and/or profession of
coaching will have at least some of these traits, or at least
one of these traits. But time and again, you will be
disappointed.

Our Coaching Reality

Most coaches are fat, stubborn, and arrogant
Neanderthals who are clinging to some long ago high
school glory that was as short-lived as they are short-
tempered. But resumes matter in sports. If you are
coaching in the same town where you threw a 1-hitter in
high school, or even were just a well-known (if not well-
liked) jock, then you have a remarkable license to train
and nurture the next generation of kids. Logic doesn't
seem to play into it. Watch Danny McBride as Kenny
Powers in *Eastbound and Down* on TV if you aren't
familiar with the phenomenon.

Conversations with these coaches go like this:

> **You:** *"Hey, Coach, I just wanted to let you know that as we will be coming back from my mother's funeral on Saturday, Sam may be just a few minutes late for warm-ups."*
>
> **Coach:** *"If he's late, he has to sit out the first half."*
>
> **You:** *"But he's never been late before, and other kids are late all the time and they don't sit."*
>
> **Coach:** *"That's the rule, nothing I can do about it."*

~

> **You:** *"Hi, Coach, um, my name is Ted Williams and of course you know my son Ted Williams Jr. Anyway, I was just wondering — Ted went 2 for 2 last game and also in the three games before that, even though he only plays three innings. Do you think he could possibly get a few more innings in the next game? I've noticed that there are kids who play every inning and don't have a single hit yet."*
>
> **Coach:** *"Which one is Ted?"*

Others coaches are not quite as dickish, but often make up for it with a comical/dangerous level of stupidity. Others compensate with a badly misplaced narcissism rooted in their self-assessed glory days.

Legends in Their Own Mind

We had a hockey coach when my son was 11 that was a classic. Before each practice he would sit in the locker room shirtless, with his enormous belly protruding out over his sweats like a prize-winning pumpkin at the fair, and then ever so slowly undertake the task of getting his skates on. At this age, the kids still had moms in and out of the locker room; fetching equipment, tying skates, or just generally fussing over their children. So they were treated to this spectacle at every practice. And you could kind of tell that he hoped maybe they thought it was kind of hot. Like here is this former high school hockey legend just chillin' like a villin', half naked, before he takes the ice to tell their boys how it is.

When the movie *Miracle*, about the 1980 Olympic Gold Medal team, came out, this coach told the players that he might have made that team if he had a little more heart. Given the fact that he didn't even attend a regional tryout, much less the national tryout, it makes me wonder how he came to this conclusion. A little more heart — and a whole butt-load more talent maybe?

When we did our little end-of-year banquet where he talked about each of the players, he kept saying, *"The coaches and I called him [nickname] because he was always [doing something that made the nickname fit."* The funny thing was, the only nicknames he had were "Assassin" (evidently for goal scorers) and "Digger" (for kids willing to go battle pucks out of the corner). So every kid would be introduced and he would say "and we call him Digger," either forgetting or not caring that he had already said the same thing about four or five other kids.

Logic Does Not Play Into It

More often than not, the coach's kid is one of the better players. This is not coincidence. Coaches are usually former jocks and jocks beget jocks. So that's fine because even though they get more playing time than they actually deserve, they are better than most of the alternatives. But, as with everything, we have the exceptions.

I remember one kid, Bill Nebber, whose dad was my Babe Ruth baseball coach. Now Bill played catcher, which had always been my position. I suddenly found myself in right field, three innings a game. I wasn't the greatest ballplayer on earth by this point; damn if I could hit that pitching once the kids started shaving. But defensively at least, I was still passable (though, it dawns on me now that this may not be the right adjective for a catcher. Let's say *serviceable*). And, holy mother of God, that coach's kid was totally fucking hopeless. For some reason it was one of those seasons where we had lots and lots of plays at the plate. Evidentially, our pitching was yielding plenty of shots to the deep grass, but our outfielders had good arms and the runners kept testing us over and over. Time and again the throw would come, on time and on target. There would be Bill, waiting with the runner still 10 steps from home. And *fwlappp* off his big mitt it would go, skidding to the fence, bringing in another runner or two behind. But his dad was the coach, and this never seemed to discourage Coach that he had the right guy back there.

Accepting the Inevitable

And so in the end, you will have to coach. You simply won't be able to tolerate another minute with these monkeys. It's too painful. And stop right now with the "*I*

34

don't have time" and "*My job is way too demanding*" excuses and the "*I've never coached before*" nonsense.

There are two reasons you will coach:

1. **Playing Time**: Nobody gets the PT or the sweet positions like the coach's kid, and for this reason alone you will have to do it.

2. **Simple Decency**: The alternative is some boob with all the sports sense of your mother-in-law's left boob who not only cannot recognize your son's obvious talent, but has the people skills, communication skills, and personal hygiene of a rutting hedgehog. So that leaves you to save not only yourself but the rest of humanity from his migraine-inducing decisions all season.

And do not think that you will compromise by being an assistant coach! I will not allow it. It will only marginally address reason one, and two not at all.

Your Play:

Volunteer to coach. Usually, this is granted with undisguised gratitude. But where exceptions exist, kiss some commissioner ass.

Get a whistle. Memorize the next chapter.

Chapter 6: Coaching

How Hard Can It Be?

Extremely hard as it turns out. But don't worry about it because by the time you figure that out, it will be too late anyway. To arm you for your coaching journey, let's start with some simple rules:

Rule #1 The coach is always right.

Rule #2 If the coach is wrong, refer to rule #1.

These are important rules, because despite surprising even yourself by becoming the most enlightened, fair, effective, inspiring, and downright fucking awesome coach since Coach Taylor of the Dillon Panthers,[4] inexplicably there will actually be parents who do not share this view. In fact, there may be *several* parents who do not share this view. Actually, probably all the parents will not share this view. And they will not hesitate to clarify for their sons that, since you're basically an idiot, their sons don't really need to show you respect either. So this will make your job slightly harder. Thus, the rules.

---

[4] And let's just stop right here if you don't get the reference. For the love of Christ, put down the book, get on Netflix and rent all five seasons of *Friday Night Lights* and watch it straight through in one glorious, insane weekend fueled by coffee, Mountain Dew, and Alamo Freeze burgers. Then resume reading.

More Rules:

Rule #3: Parents are Not Your Allies

Parents should, as a rule, be assumed to be your enemy until proven otherwise. They just want what you want: more playing time for their kid, but they aren't willing to put in the time as coach to get it. Furthermore, they know nothing about the game's finer points the way you do. Try to dazzle them with your command of the game and then shun them so that they do not feel comfortable offering their opinion about anything. Tell everyone that you will be trying to get everyone equal playing time and an opportunity to play all the different positions. In reality, it should be a strict meritocracy where the kids with the hottest moms get the most playing time.

Try this helpful role-play in the event that you are approached by a parent:

> **Parent:** *"Hi, Coach, great game last night. That was fantastic the way we came back at the end. I think you played it just perfectly by calling that time out and then pulling the goalie with three minutes left. Nobody saw that coming!"*
>
> **You:** *"Thank you."*
>
> **Parent:** *"Can Sam get a little more playing time?"*
>
> **You**: *"No."*

Rule #4: Separate the Wheat from the Chaff
The best little players out there are also the best little
people. This may not seem obvious right away. The less
talented kids will be respectful and polite. They have to
be because having been cursed with genetically inferior
looks, size, and athletic acumen, they have to find other
ways to compensate, such as having a positive attitude,
good manners, and a respectful demeanor. Meanwhile,
the talented players will have been handed to them most
of what they wanted in life and will behave in a spoiled
and pouty manner as a consequence. Despite this seeming
paradox, you will warm to the talented and come to
loathe the untalented.

Why? Because the bad ones will trot out to the plate, time
after time, and strike out! Or they will simply let the
grounder go through their legs, again. Or they will
dribble the ball off their foot, over and over, just as sure
as the sun will rise in the east — and you will hate them
for it. So do not waste your valuable time trying to like
them, support them, or help them with their swing.
Marginalize them and hasten the day when they decide
that the school play holds more charm for them than a
double-play (which they will never experience anyway).
You will be doing them, and the wider community, a
great Darwinian service.

**Rule #5: Winning Isn't Everything, It's the Only
Thing**
Forget the whole "*if you had fun, you won*" crap right
now because it's crap. If you had fun **and** you scored at

least one more point than the other team — then you won. Or, put another way, if you lost, I can pretty much guaranfuckingtee you that you did not have fun. Winning is what our entire species is based on and you, my friend, are not going to change a billion years of evolutionary success with some cheery platitudes to your team. And guess what? The parents will like you much more as a coach if you win. And, helpfully, they won't be as inclined to argue about the relative minutes their kid got vs. yours because everyone is too happy with the win to worry about it. But if you lose, well then every little detailed gripe they have about you is now validated with the glaring shame of failure.

Your players will like you better too, and they might actually do what you tell them on occasion. Your assistants will like you. The umps and refs will like you. The newspaper will like you. The rec department staff and the Zamboni driver will like you. The league will defer to you. The moms on your team, and on the other teams, will want to make babies with you.

A softball coach friend of mine once had a little girl ask him why they were going out in the field for a 5th inning. Games were six innings long in this league, so you wouldn't expect this to come as a surprise to her. Problem was, his team was so bad that they usually ended their games in the 4th inning with the 10-run deficit "Mercy Rule." Thus, you could forgive the little girl's confusion and surprise. But not her sorry play.

Your Play:

Winning is where you want to be. That's home.

More Tips for the Coach:
There is simply so much to know. Keep reading.

The Team Mom
Get one. There is a surprising amount of administrative drudgery to coaching that should be hastily offloaded to this affable and highly organized individual. Do not take the first volunteer or pick the one that you secretly entertain locker room fantasies about. Carefully screen for that generous spirit with boundless energy, patience and a willingness to spend hours on the phone if a rain-out requires a complicated reschedule. Hold out for a freakish gift for spreadsheets, fundraising, organizing potlucks and ability to negotiate scarce ice time with rink managers. You will thank me for this. You're welcome.

Your Play:

Look for a MILP (Mom I would Like to Pay) - she is that good at organizing stuff.

The Weird Kid
Kids are great, if they are your own, and even then only within limits. But most other people's kids are really annoying little turds full of questions, irritating habits, unpleasant smells, and medical problems.

I had a kid on one of my hockey teams who threw up at every single practice. I'm not making this up. I had to clean up vomit in the locker room, around the rink, on the bench, on the ice (have you ever seen frozen vomit? Very hard to clean), and just about everywhere he went. I finally had to tell his parents, "Look, no offense, but I'm trying to coach a team here. Unless you can bring a medical team and janitorial service to every practice with him, I think you should leave him home."

Every team also has that one kid who can best be described as ... particularly odd. All the kids are weird. The odd kid is the one who all the other weird kids think is weird. Weird squared as it were. They are really intelligent but have no idea how to relate to other 10-year-old kids because they just aren't wired with the usual brain matter of cheese whiz. They are instead quirky, smart, and have a large vocabulary. They are aware of current events. So they will quickly try to attach themselves to you, the adult, with super glue because they hope you might be polite enough to listen to their stream of consciousness blather, which the other kids and their parents long ago stopped doing.

Your Play:

Shun the weird kid.

An Adolescent Mind is a Terrible Thing to Waste (your time on)
Kids are like that dog from the movie *Up* when he sees a squirrel ... *"SQUIRREL!!!"* They are not like you and me. They cannot, even if their very lives depended on it, execute an entire basketball play from start to finish

without doing something totally stupid and unnecessary in the middle of it.

So approaching them like another ordinary human being is a rookie coach mistake.

It's important that you make them fear you. This comes in handy in a variety of ways. Number one, they won't talk to you anymore (except the weird kid, who has no one else to talk to and may actually be smart enough to see through your game). Number two, they are less likely to spill your coffee.

This can be a major problem: coffee spillage. I would always show up to baseball games with a hot mug of unnecessarily expensive "Coach Roast" coffee. It was my little caffeine oasis that I could nurse for about 45 minutes of happiness during what is otherwise the interminable pre-game routines. But every time I would put it down in the dugout some cretin would manage to knock it over with his mitt, arms, legs, or ass — and then just leave it. They wouldn't even set it back up right with its now diminished contents, probably because they didn't even realize they had knocked it over, such is the degree of their self-absorption. So finally, I staged a very loud and frightening bat-and-equipment-throwing exhibition concerning the almost religious sanctity and respect that should be afforded the coach's coffee. This seemed to accomplish what their apparent lack of parenting had not.

Your Play:

Establish fear. Once done, you will be afforded a *modicum* of respect that can be leveraged in the form of getting them to line up or pick equipment up or do some other unpleasant tasks.

Note: this respect still stops well short of getting them to follow your words with enough intellectual attention such that they could actually execute a motion offense, a nickel defense, or comprehend the nuances of proper base-running strategy.

So it's important to stay realistic.

Assistant Coaches – Your Man Friday
To reiterate: You will not be an assistant. It's all the time commitment without the not-inconsiderable reward of being lord of all you survey. Admittedly, being lord of a bunch of barely civilized little people is not quite the same as being Julius Caesar or George Clooney, but compared to your home and work life, it may feel a little like it at times. Want them to jog around the field so that you can get another two minutes of peace before starting practice? Just issue the command. Want one of the more irritating young lads to crawl into the net and retrieve the 57 pucks you just shot in there? Say the word. It's fun. But as assistant, there is much less opportunity for this sort of Napoleonic excess.

So you will be the head coach and you will carefully select your assistants from the group of guys that has volunteered to do it. And, generally, this list will only have one name on it, such is the enthusiasm for this post. So you will just have to take him on.

But if you *do* get to choose, or have to recruit because not a soul raised his hand, then really, the only requirement is that they have an excellent sense of humor. You will be doing the strategic thinking and thinking of big thoughts; this person's function is to hit ground balls to the left side, pick up cones after a drill, buy beer after practice, and, most of all, make you laugh by ridiculing the kids behind their backs.

Your Play:

Make it understood right off that you don't want any suggestions from your assistants. No speeches after your speeches, or anything else of that nature.

Tell them that you are busy and need them to take the head job for one game, but make sure that it is the toughest game on the schedule so that they will lose and you can maintain your air of strategic superiority.

Inspirational Speeches – Your Sweat Stained Soap Box

Speeches are as essential to the coaching quiver as Tums and beer. Kids are sitting there, nervous, anxious, and lost before the big game. They are looking to you, their leader, to fill their heads with knowledge and to fill their hearts with the courage of lions. They need a vision, a rallying cry, and a way forward out of the darkness that is their pre-game uncertainty.

Did that persuade you? I didn't think so. It was pure crap. And it's fair to say that the hundreds of speeches and

44

speechlets that I've given over the years were similarly devoid of value and, therefore, locker room impact. Giving detailed game instruction to young kids is about as promising as explaining to your cat that you don't want it barfing up hairballs in your sock drawer anymore.

But the thing is: You still have to give speeches. Why?

A. Because it's expected;

B. Because how else are you going to fill that time? and

C. How many other times in your life are you going to have a locker room full of kids listening to you (well, okay, pretending to) and get to live out a life-long movie role fantasy. These moments must be savored.

Your Play:

Memorize and deploy the following speeches:

The All Purpose Speech
This can be used whenever you are bored, virtually asleep, or just don't have the faintest idea what else to say:

> *"Let's just take this game one quarter at a time. Play your game. Work together and focus on teamwork. We are better than these guys and we know it. Now we just have to go out there and show it. Don't worry about the calls, just play*

smart and the score will take care of itself. Okay, hands in, everyone on three — Go, Mudpuppies!"

Lost Cause
Self-explanatory:

> *"Okay, ladies, I'm not going to sugar coat this thing. These gals can outplay us in every facet of the game. They can walk faster than we can run. They have outscored their opponents by a combined score of 500 to 3 and they will probably sleep with your boyfriends tonight. We have no chance. That said ... I want you gals to hold your heads up and get out there and show them some Porcupine Pride! Let's go, Porcs!"*

Half Time
Lots of time to kill here so it requires a mixture of inspiration and tactics:

> *"Okay, let's huddle up. Hey great job men. Really, superb. Now we just need to curtail some of the mistakes. Henderson — when you call for a fair catch, you actually have to subsequently **catch the ball**. Perkins — too many holding calls; I lost count at 15. Caveman — once the kid is down on the ground and the whistle has blown, you can't kick them or do **anything at all to them**, especially not gouge out their eyes. I don't think I've ever even seen a 90-yard penalty before. So let's try to fix that stuff and I think we will really*

46

come out strong in the second half. Put your
hands in on three."

Time Out with Seconds to Go

"Gentlemen, desperate times call for desperate
measures.

Spaulding — get me Billy Baroo!

No, just kidding. Flanderson — get me my cattle
prod."

One other thing: Do not make the mistake of saying your
piece and letting its awesomeness hang in the air like
Shakespeare's *Henry the Fifth* before the Battle of
Agincourt only to lay a turd on it by asking your assistant
coach if he has anything to add. I can guarantee you that
what he adds will wipe those little tears of devotion and
promised glory right off their tiny faces. And for God's
sake, under no circumstances ever, ever allow the team
mom to weigh in. This might seem like a far-fetched
thing to caution you against, but I'm still scarred by one
of my son's hockey teams, where the head coach would
bore the kids for about three minutes; followed by the
first assistant, who would assault them politely for
another two; followed by the second assistant, who would
rhetorically murder them for another three minutes; and
finally Team Mom, Mrs. Nichols, would smother their
little souls with 120 excruciating seconds of complete,

nonsensical gibberish. By the time they took the ice they were in a complete coma.

Chapter 7: Adventures in Coaching

What Doesn't Kill You Will Leave You Wounded

There's really no manual for doing this. And even if there were, would you read it? Guys who read instruction manuals are not really guys' guys, if you know what I mean. *Playbooks*, on the other hand...

Poor Preparation - When (and when not) to Improvise

A few years ago I was coaching Babe Ruth fall baseball. It had rained overnight but I hadn't really registered that before showing up for our game the next morning. By the time I realized that the field really wasn't playable, the other team was already arriving from about 45 minutes away and I didn't have the heart to call it. So I resolved to get the field playable. But the baselines were not just muddy, they were a form of liquid goo that I could only describe as K-Y jelly mixed with snot. So attempts to rake and put a little Dry Fit or whatever they had in the shed on there was a little like trying to get dog poop off your shoe with a Q-tip.

So I ran to the store and bought about nine bags of kitty litter. Worked like a charm, up to a point. The funny thing about kitty litter is that after it does its job absorbing moisture, it basically hardens to a form of gritty cement. Not a big problem if you're not worried about a little adolescent blood loss due to nasty abrasions suffered by sliding over a belt sander (I wasn't). But a bigger problem when the head grounds guy finds out what you've done the next day; I had to move to a new state as part of the Federal Coach Protection Program. These things happen.

Respect – Clawing Your Way up the Food Chain
Shortly after moving back to Vermont from Minnesota and after deciding that I *definitely* wasn't going to coach hockey again (too busy with my new job, and thinking up practice drills is too boring), I got a call from the league president saying that my son had been placed on a C team (lowest of three tiers) and that they didn't have a coach. Here's what went down. They had enough boys at the C level for two teams; the policy is to divide the talent between those two teams equally. But the *other* team already had a coach, and he had used his influence to stack his team. I don't mean tilted in his favor, I mean he had every single good player (and with that, all the type of dads willing to be a coach or assistant coach. I think he had two assistants lined up already). Needing a coach for the rejects, the president went down the list of all the dads, asking if they would coach. All said no. Evidently, he didn't consider me a prospect. So as the only name on the list that he hadn't approached, he didn't ask me if I would *coach* but if I would just babysit the kids for a few practices while they dangled a small stipend of a few hundred dollars out there to get a "professional" coach (i.e. someone who won't do it for free because they don't have a kid on the team, but is otherwise about as qualified as the school bus driver).

So here's what he was saying to me in a nutshell:

1. We've placed your son on the worst team possible.

2. We don't consider you worthy of a job that we've asked every other living human being to take, all of whom have turned it down, but we *would* like you to help us out anyway, just not with any actual hockey coaching.

3. Our solution for these boys who are already going to lose every game is to give them a journeyman coach who may show up occasionally and who really doesn't give a shit.

This really chapped my heinie because I had already coached for four seasons in MINNESOTA, cradle of hockey greatness in the lower 48, and by God if I didn't take my last Pee-Wee team all the way to the Twin Cities District Finals on a true Cinderella run, beating four *much* better teams on the way there.

> *"Excuse me, but where am I now? Vermont? And I'm not worthy to coach your crappy C team?"*

The president didn't know my coaching resume, and was a very nice guy, but it still grated to be cast in such a sorry light.

So this was my response:

1. I'm your new head coach. You're welcome.

2. We're going to get together with the other C coach who took all the good players and have a little discussion about that.

We met at the rink. The other coach was great. He was another local legend but bummed he was coaching at the C Level. And here I was, trying to make matters worse by taking away some of his ringers. Not being in the local hockey fraternity, it was clear that he viewed me as some sort of single-celled organism and curtly informed me that the teams were even. I curtly informed him that he was full of shit and we went a few rounds like that. In the end he had all the leverage, but I managed to get one player — luckily a good one. That kid plus my son put up about 30 points between them for the year. I also was able to get pretty good play out of the rest of my cast offs, and we went all the way to the quarter-finals in the state tournament, leaving the other coach and his considerably more talented group behind when they bowed out almost immediately.

If you think this then righted my reputation as a coach within the local organization, you would be sadly mistaken. But it still felt good.

Your Play:

Never use kitty litter for anything except for its intended purpose of deodorizing sneakers.

Do not confuse actual coaching experience with local rink cred.

Chapter 8: The Boys' Locker Room

The 9th Circle of Hell

I have only been in a women's locker once. And it was not in the manner I would choose it, which would be as the Invisible Man. Rather; it was in a state of post treadmill delirium at the club where I just innocently wandered a few feet in before coming to my senses and well before seeing the frolicking shower scene that was undoubtedly underway just beyond view.

I have scarcely more experience with Men's locker rooms because I make a point of spending so little time in them. They are exactly as you picture them if you have not had the pleasure: moldy, damp and always populated with that dumpy naked guy standing directly in front of the locker you put your crap in.

But longer spells in boy's locker rooms were an occupational hazard of the basketball and particularly the hockey coach. And I am thusly well versed in their particular sub-culture.

We like to think that the field of play is where the learning and character development take place. But there is an equal, if not greater amount of knowledge that is gleaned by your young man in the sweaty, smelly, and largely unsupervised man-cave of the locker room. Certainly their first exposure to the filthiest words, jokes, and descriptions of sexual congress will come in this temple of soiled laundry and sin. Also, the rapier wit of the most-clever will be honed to a fine point on the whetstone of shower-steamed trash talk. And finally, the pranks and practical jokes will flourish like mushrooms under a rotting log (or under a hockey locker room bench).

Bad Words
Heard first in the locker room:

- Cleveland Steamer[5]
- Santorum[6]
- Rim Job[7]

Bad Jokes
I am not endorsing the following jokes. I am simply offering them as representative of the locker room genre.

Three guys go to a ski lodge, and there aren't enough rooms, so they have to share a bed. In the middle of the night, the guy on the right wakes up and says, *"I had this wild, vivid dream of getting a hand job!"* The guy on the left wakes up and, unbelievably, he's had the same dream. Then the guy in the middle wakes up and says, *"That's funny, I dreamed I was skiing!"*

~

A minister is checking into a hotel and says to the receptionist, "I certainly hope that the porn channel in my

---

[5] Aha, you were hoping that I would provide the meaning down here in the footnote, weren't you?
[6] No dice. But the other meaning is the last name of the guy from Pennsylvania that ran for president.
[7] Actually, I don't really know what they mean. The kids wouldn't say.

room is disabled." The receptionist replies, "No, of course not, you sick fuck, it's just regular porn."

Bad Smells
Start with curdled milk. Place it in a sauna. Add tuna mixed with cat turds. Stir. Bake at 400 degrees for 300 years and you're getting close to a hockey locker room.

Fun Pranks
Locker room pranks are legion.

On my nephew's swim team a new prank known as "spearing" became popular. As the name might imply (or might not), it involved using your extended fingers as a spear to drive between the butt cheeks of an unsuspecting swimmer who was passing by, fresh from the shower with a terry cloth towel wrapped around their midsection.

According to my nephew, this mildly painful and exceptionally shocking weapon was deployed with a degree of tit-for-tat between the unwary and the off-their-guard teammates for a few weeks, until one kid feeling rather injured by the experience (probably more from embarrassment than pain, but perhaps both if it was a particularly well-delivered jab) reported the incident to his parents. His parents (or their lawyer) then concluded that a sexual assault had taken place and pretty soon one swimmer was brought up on charges. It cost his parents many thousands of dollars in legal fees before he was eventually acquitted, which is probably good since he wasn't even the kid that actually did it. To his enduring credit, he did not finger (my word choice) the guy who did. And let's face it, more egregiously painful and humiliating acts have befallen the average fraternity pledge.

Still, there is a moral to this story for kids: When spearing, get verbal consent first, wear a hand condom, and lawyer up hard at the first sign of trouble. This is really just common sense.

Your Play:

Enter a boy's locker room at your own risk. Armor up like you are an aid worker in a sub-Saharan Ebola clinic: gown, gloves and mask.

Chapter 9: The Sports Dad

A Man for All Seasons

You won't always be the coach. Unjust as this is, by the time your kid reaches high school, they generally already have those positions filled. In fact, it's a paid position, believe it or not. And here you have been doing it for free all this time. Oops.

Anyway, these other guys and gals have those jobs (and a level of job security that would make a teamster blush) and you don't, so you will have to release your young charges into their care and unsteadily find your way back to the bleachers with the rest of the angry mob. It can be a rocky adjustment. You're used to a certain status by this time, which primarily frees you from having to know the common folk or listen to their opinions about things. Welcome back.

There are four primary types of sports dad that you should be aware of and ready to defend yourself against:

Smug Dad

Smug Dad dresses well. He can afford to. He has good hair and a young wife that is probably not related to his son or daughter. He won't ever bother to learn your name, nor acknowledge that he even knows you. Smug Dad's kid can play. He wouldn't show up if it were otherwise. He views your existence as just an inconvenience necessitated by the fact that his very talented son or daughter needs teammates to help accentuate their superior skill level, even if said teammates have to be your offspring. They only stick around until sophomore or junior year when the prodigies head off to prep school to prepare for Princeton. If you compliment their child's play after the game, they will merely reply "thank you."

Your Play:

Try to goad him. Sit nearby and, just loudly enough to be overheard, say things about their kid like:

> *"Mikala is so strong on the point. I just hope that we can get through the playoffs before her pregnancy starts showing and slowing her down."*

> *"Trey looks a little slower out there than usual. I wonder if it has anything to do with the beer weight he's been putting on."*

Red Neck Dad

- **Height**: 5'10"
- **Weight**: 270 lbs.
- **Build**: stocky working on flabby
- **Diet**: Red Meat
- **Politics**: Red Meat
- **Car**: Hummer H2

- **Quotes**: "Did you see my boy take out #15?" and "Let the kids play!" (yelled at the ref when his son fouls out again)
- **Wonders**: If he should start his son on steroids yet
- **Secret Wish**: That he could wear eye black to games without getting laughed at

Your Play:

When confronted with Red Neck Dad, just say "hey, nice Hummer!"

Fish Out of Water Dad

These are the non-sports guys. Somehow a recessive gene, or one from the wife, has slipped into the mix and their child is into sports, despite no encouragement from anyone. Fish Out of Water Dad is an attorney who plays tenor sax on weekends with an amateur jazz group and has had a screenplay about John Coltrane in the works for over a decade. He has been to some Super Bowl parties but spent the entire time in the kitchen chatting up some of the similarly disinterested guests about how barbaric the blood sport of football is. He shows up to games, or some of them, because he is part of the parenting generation where that's what you do (and he's more than a little afraid of his wife), but he is glued to his cell phone, doesn't have a clue what the rules are, and frequently arrives very late or not at all due to work conflicts.

Your Play:

Try to score a little free legal advice from him during half time.

Crazy Dad

Crazy Dad can yell so loudly at the refs that they can actually be heard over the glass of a hockey rink, past the crappy acoustics, above the general din of cheering fans, and into the ears of a ref skating 100 feet away from them — and with sufficient animus that the ref will stop the game, point to the offender and order them out of the rink. This is a class IV move. It's hard for a normal person to achieve even if you were trying to.

Crazy Dad will approach a coach with a complaint or crazy suggestion, during a game. Crazy Dad will run up and down the sidelines shouting instructions to their soccer player, who is 9. Crazy Dad will yell sophomoric things at umps like "IF YOU HAD ONE MORE EYE YOU WOULD BE A CYCLOPS!!!" And Crazy Dad will even scream at opposing fans with a look in his eye somewhere between Jim Carrey and Charlie Manson.

Crazy Dad is flat out, bat shit, *crazy*.

Your Play:

A wide berth, obviously. Wave, smile, and beeline it for the far end of the bleachers.

Chapter 10: The Hockey (etc.) Mom

Pitbull with Lipstick

Moms love sports, especially when their offspring are on the field of battle. With the exception of Crazy Dad, there is no louder or more outraged fan when the call goes the wrong way. Opposing coaches are the scum of the earth as well because, obviously, they are teaching their kids nothing but cheap shots and dirty tricks. And God help the opposing player who gets in any sort of fracas with their prodigal son or daughter. They would have that other kid locked up on Devil's Island with no trial.

There is another side to all this, however. That is a truly and spectacularly appalling level of ignorance about the games themselves, not only in terms of the basic rules but more significantly with how the game is properly played. In the early years of youth soccer, you will hear an absolute chorus of moms screaming, *"BOOT IT, ASHLEY!!!"* and *"NICE KICK, DAVID."* No amount of observation seems to alert them to the fact that simply kicking the ball forward in soccer does no good at all and is, in fact, basically a turnover. Worse, their unbridled enthusiasm and volume has a very detectible impact on getting the kids to do just that, much to the coach's irritation (or delight, if the coach shares a similar level of ignorance, as is too often the case).

This applies to all sports right up through high school where they take the thinnest possible knowledge of the game and turn it in to loudly shrieked platitudes:

"Great hit, Jeff!"

(Yelled in reference to a sharp grounder hit
straight to short resulting in a 6-4-3 double play.)

"Hey, what's that????"

(Shrieked to a hockey ref after a perfectly legal
and unassailable check leaves one of their players
on the ice.)

"Good try, Jill!"

(Exclaimed in response to a forced brick thrown
up from the cheap seats when a teammate was
wide open under the net.)

There is another species within the sports mom genus as
well: the *know-it-all mom*. They either played themselves
or have earnestly picked up a bit of the insider lingo
along the way. Their trick is to sit with the other parents
and call out detailed instructions to the kids in a calmer
more measured tone that plainly demonstrates their
superior level of sports knowledge to everyone else. It's
clearly audible to all the assembled parents, and not even
remotely to the kids.

Examples:

Soccer: *"Settle, Missy"* and *"Square, Caitlin."*

Lax: *"Slide, Connor"* and *"Nice split dodge,
Jeff."*

Hockey: *"Coach, we need to get more pressure
on the puck!"*

Moms are also far less timid than dads when it comes to
confronting coaches about whatever it is they feel may be

adversely affecting their child's psyche. This may be because they have boobs and are therefore used to getting men to do what they want.

They will stroll right up to the coach and say:

"Why isn't Michael playing more?"

The coach is *thinking* to himself ... well ... because:

A. Michael is horrible. A complete liability out there and probably a danger to himself and to others...and

B. He hates basketball and told me that he doesn't want to play, ever...and

C. I've already had him in twice

But instead the coach will actually say, *"He's going in next."*

Your Play:

Advocacy: It works. At least it does if you have boobs. So get your wife to talk to coaches.

Arrive late to games so you can position your folding chair as far from the know-it-all mom as possible. You cannot escape the others. There is no play there.

Chapter 11: Envy

The 10th Commandment

It's right there in the good book:

"Thou shalt not covet thy neighbour's wife, nor his manservant, nor his maidservant, nor his ox, nor his ass, nor any thing that is thy neighbour's."

And that pretty well covers it. Yet, still, you *will* be tempted to covet thy neighbor's kid's curveball, 50-yard time, or 3-point shot, and probably more so than his manservant is my guess, though perhaps less than his ox.

You will know envy. Despite your best efforts, despite your passable genetics (and I am being charitable here), despite all the long hours of extra drills at the park and inspirational speeches, you will wish you kid could play like *that* kid.

Sometimes, as was the case with one of my son's hockey teammates in Minnesota, it's just simple lineage. Dad was an NHL winger (as was *his* dad) and sure enough if this little 7-year-old couldn't already skate with the power and finesse of a high school senior. What can you say?

Other times, it will be more mysterious. The kid is 6'2" and has the hand-eye coordination of Bruce Lee. Then your gaze wanders to his mom: short and squat; more chimichanga than cheetah. Clearly not a former jock. And you will look at the dad: similar story, receding hairline, small hands, shorter than mom, and looks like he might lose to his wife in a cage match — and you think to yourself ... how in the *hell* did that happen? It's not right. It's not fair.

And of course you are right. It's not, and it isn't.

Your Play:

Attempt to get your child born at the same hospital at the same time as Tom Brady's kid, and make the switch.

Or, read the next chapter.

Chapter 12: Magic Elixirs

How to Buy Your Way Out of It

Once despair has left you again, usually after the third or fourth cup of coffee in my case, you redouble your efforts to help your son or daughter improve, which is to say: You try to buy your way out of it.

The Answer is Money. What was the question?
This is how youth sports works too. We can't help it. Deep down, we all think:

"What if? Maybe Coach Doubleday's $250 summer batting clinic is all that stands between my son and batting third next spring for the JV team or, dare I say it, Varsity ...? And then the accolades and the girls and the vindication for the shame I felt in ninth grade when Coach Barnacle benched me and my life began its inexorable swirl down the toilet will begin."

Money can fix this! And you've got your wallet out faster than the No. 9 hitter on your Little League team makes a trip to the plate and back.

There must be an edge out there! Private coaches, X3000 core training machines, those little lopsided balls they sell at Dick's Sporting Goods that you're supposed to bounce back and forth to improve coordination, a new bat made out of rare Peruvian Kevlar that is illegal in all 50 states, a shooting sleeve, a DVD series guaranteed to improve your shooting form, protein drinks, and prayer. This last one is actually free if pursued at home, but, in my experience, is also the least effective.

There is a very large industry (and seemingly about 15 separate golf magazine titles) built around our inherent optimism that with just a little more information, tips, diagrams, or tools anyone can be a better athlete. This is, of course, a huge lie to sell golf magazines and other expensive stuff but how do you know that for sure?

Camps –It's Fun to Play at the YMCA
Over the years, we have invested, conservatively, in no less than three dozen camps of one type or another; hockey, basketball, lacrosse, baseball, cross country, curling, etc. Each one has set us back somewhere between $300 to $1,000. It adds up. And results? Well, results may vary. I wish I could say that after each one, or after even just one, I thought to myself, *"Wow, I think he's really turned the corner with his shooting or ball handling or shoe tying,"* but the truth is I've always just thought, *"Wow, I just spent 600 bucks and I can't tell any difference."*

But obviously it never stopped me from doing it again. Maybe it just wasn't the *right* camp. As I said, hope springs eternal.

Equipment – A Little Thing I Call Marketing (or a Mitt made by Mitt Romney)
For the first 150 years of hockey's existence, you bought your stick at a five and dime, a hardware store, or sporting goods store that had more hunting gear than hockey sticks. They were fairly simple implements made of wood that set you back about $14. Baseball bats and most other types of equipment were similar. This era

lasted a surprisingly long time. The dam broke when Nike discovered that the more they charged for the new signature shoes of their hot new hoops star Michael Jordan, the more people wanted them, rather than the usual reverse equation that had held since the invention of the barter system. Despite this insight and the rapid proliferation of $100-plus basketball shoes, the largely backward, Canadian dominated, hockey equipment world carried on for quite a period of time, still believing that they should build quality sticks and sell them for $10 to $20 because, well, they only cost about $5 to make. This seemed logical enough to your basic Canuck.

> *"Eh, Bob, I think this stick costs aboot $5 to make. Let's sell it for $10 and we'll have about $7 left to buy beer, eh?"*

> *"Okaaay, Doug. Good ideeer. Now let's go play hockey. Take off."*

And so on. But as these things go, some sharp MBAs at Bain Capital noticed that these companies were still family owned and undervalued. So they bought them, consolidated them, leveraged them, de-leveraged them, found synergies, and flipped them. And during all that, they brought in the big marketing guns from the coast to do what they do.

Your Play:

Get out there and buy that hockey stick that weighs less than a paperclip and has a completely awesome paint job on it. Your kid will still not be any better at hockey and you will be short about $250 (assuming you bought on sale) but Mitt Romney will be $20 richer.

Chapter 13: Travel Teams

Going Down the Road Feeling Broke

When my older son was just 6 years old and in his first year of Mite Hockey, I noticed a gentleman who was trolling around the rink looking for "talent." He was forming an "elite" team of players to play spring hockey at tournaments around Minnesota. Of course my first thought was, "Why isn't he talking to me?" Alex's D1 potential (Minnesota or BC?) seemed clearly evident to me. But then I do have a better eye than most.

Anyway, after I got over the fact that he wasn't going to talk to me (okay, I'm still not over it), I began to think, "*Really? These kids are 6!*" They are still many years away from growing testicles, nose hair, or any of the other harbingers of puberty that would actually begin to suggest whether there was true hockey potential there; and yet here we are, separating the wheat from the chaff already.

Pathetic and awful on the one hand, but also time to get the kid into camps, start working on dry land, aerobic conditioning, weights,[8] and film sessions so he doesn't get left behind. Because it's an escalator, right? You need to be on the one that leads to the hardware department, not the one going to linens.

---

[8] Where do you start them weight-wise for bench press at this age?

And so began our journey into traveling teams. Some of them are truly elite and difficult to make, of course, but there are always plenty of others available for those who simply have the backing of a parental checkbook. We were usually on those teams.

AAU basketball tournaments are about as absurd from a cost-benefit ratio as you are likely to find. Somehow, I was convinced to spend many thousands of dollars a season on team fees, uniforms, gym time, gas, hotels, and meals to get in a paltry handful of games.

A typical weekend would go something like this:

1. Get up at the crack of dawn on Saturday and drive 250 miles to Boston or Albany or Rochester. Buy breakfast and lunch on the road.
2. Arrive at the Schenectady Central High School the prescribed 60 minutes before game time, pay your $16 for the entry fee for you and the wife, and watch a mind-numbing 35-to-5 rout finish up between two 12-and-under girls teams on your court.
3. Play your first game and lose badly because your little Vermont team can't begin to compete with the elite select programs of these larger, denser, and seemingly more talented cities.
4. Wonder to yourself why the coach played the kid so much who shoots first and thinks not at all.
5. Wait another interminable two hours for your second game, killing time by visiting the snack table and perusing the bulletin board in the hallway.
6. Lose again.

7. Drive 25 minutes down the freeway past dozens of perfectly acceptable hotels to the one that the team mom inexplicably booked five towns away from the tournament. Check in and hustle out to the nearest family dining mega-chain to spend another $80 and 4,000 calories that you really didn't need after sitting on your ass all day long.
8. Watch some hotel tube, sleep too close to your wife to be comfortable but with no benefits because your son is sleeping seven feet away in the other bed.
9. Wake up to the free hotel breakfast on Sunday and some truly tragic coffee. (Seriously, how do they make it? Do they save up the bathtub water and then brew it over charcoal briquettes?)
10. Drive 25 minutes back the other way to the tournament. Wait.
11. Lose a single game in the loser's bracket, because that is what you are, and drive on home in a suicidal stupor, nearly falling asleep from the McDonald's coma you put yourself into at the last bathroom break.

Three games, maybe 45 total minutes of playing time for the kid, at about $350 a pop, not including the opportunity cost of doing absolutely anything else.

I remember one tournament in Albany, N.Y., where one of our opponents was a Nike-sponsored team. Every single kid on the team was better than the best player on the best Vermont high school team. We were facing them with a team of Vermont JV players. Our best leaper could maybe get rim with no one around and no ball in his hand. One of *their* guys dunked on us so high and hard that he got *back* rim on the jam and the ball flew about 30

71

feet back the other way up the court. So they didn't get a basket on that play, but it was cold comfort since they were already beating us about 70 to 4.

You may be thinking to yourself, well that doesn't sound very good, Tom. Maybe we'll just stick to the local stuff and school teams. Think again my friend. Hope springs eternal; you keep thinking, "Well, maybe this time." And if that isn't enough, the fact that the kids your son is competing with for next year's team are not only doing the travel team but they are also attending the overpriced camp run by the local coach, the nearby college coach, or maybe even the local legend who actually made it all the way to the pros and now runs camps using his vaunted name for marketing purposes but uses hung over college kids his business manager hired to actually coach at his camp. The Joneses are doing it all, and you just can't bring yourself to risk handicapping your guy by not trying to keep up.

So for those reasons, you will be sucked in again and again. Here's a recent experience we had with a summer "select" team that we were urged to have our son try out for by the high school coach as a way to improve off-season.

- $25 for a "tryout" at which not a single kid is cut.
- $350 team fee. Hence, the lack of cuts.
- Four practices followed by *one* tournament (all your tournament expenses are of course extra, running about $500 or more with hotels, restaurants, gas, etc.) — a real value.
- The tournament was held at a college campus in 95-degree heat without a lick of shade around the

playing fields. (Not their fault, but I just want to paint the picture here.)

- The kids were loosely divided into two squads that have never practiced as a unit before. The purpose of this was to hide from the parents until the last possible moment whether their kid was on the good squad or the bad squad. That way, no one was likely to quit before paying, because they were all under the illusion that their kid might still be on the good team. Hope springs eternal.

- Both teams were then thrown into a bracket full of teams that were about two years older and about a million times better. (Evidently the coaches couldn't be bothered to check beforehand if this tournament was the right level for our group of boys. It might have cut into profit margins to have made that phone call.)

- The games were so lopsided that in one particularly absurd contest, most of our players were told to hit the bench so that the other team could fill spots on our squad and then effectively play against themselves to make it more sporting.

- And then we drove home.

What Goes on the Road
I don't want to make it sound all bad. There is the glamour, travel, and parties to consider on these trips. Or there would be I guess, if you were traveling with an NBA team.

When on the road with the pimply faced kids, you may be based in a Best Western or something, but that's only if you're lucky. More likely you will be in a Quality Inn, Choice Inn, or any of a couple dozen other ½-star chains that dot the great American landscape. You will be right off an interstate surrounded by on ramps, 10-minute traffic signals, run-down Dairy Queens, Jiffy Lubes, self-storage facilities, and Red Lobsters. The hallway carpet will have disconcerting stains on the ground floor that probably had police tape around them the week before. Your non-smoking room will smell like Marge Simpson's sisters have recently entertained there. The pool area (always a requirement for any team booking) will be roughly the size of a pool *table* and smell so richly of chlorine that you don't have to even swim in it to have your hair turn green. The fitness room is generally the size of a New York City one-room loft's closet.

But the other parents are crazy and we usually get pretty loaded and have a blast with room parties that would do a college formal proud. Or we would, in a just world. For reasons I cannot fully explain, the parents on these teams are always about as much fun as the menu at Applebee's is exotic; the conversational equivalent of K-Mart. It's like a Mormon study group in terms of naughtiness. Of the dozens of teams we were on over the years, the most fun and *wildest,* the high water mark if you will, was the one where we wound up with about 15 adults jammed into a hotel room, a little bit drunk and being just a little too loud for that time of night such that we merited a visit from the hotel security cop. We invited him in, took the perfunctory group photo with him, and then went to bed. Not exactly Spring Break Ft. Lauderdale.

Despite this, my wife always insists that we attend all of the team functions and impromptu get-togethers because she believes that in this crucible of dull, overpriced eating, drinking, and playing in the tiny hotel pool, our

74

son is somehow forging lifelong memories, friends, and character, or something. So as soon as we arrive at the hotel, the ladies begin working on the game plan of where we're meeting for dinner, who is barbecuing in the parking lot, which room is the "kids' room" or the "parents' room," and we proceed to spend the next three or four hours boring ourselves to death. My sons, however, chips off the old block that they are, seem to prefer the hotel bed and remote control to all of this memory-making.

The partying even happens when we're not on the road and don't have the excuse of not much else to do. We parents see each other a lot already. We see each other at every game and most practices too. There are long periods of boredom involved in this where we can chat; waiting for practice to actually get out even though the coach emailed that it was supposed to be 10 minutes ago, killing time while the Zamboni circles, waiting out an interminable football half time, etc.

So we get *plenty* of face time. And yet, some do-gooder will still go ahead and announce a parents' party anyway and off we go for a full three hours of uninterrupted talk about "the kids," because that's all we have in common. Sure, you get through the perfunctory career check-off and the "what neighborhood" check-off, followed by the "do you know?" segue. But that peters out in about three minutes of conversation and then you have to find a way to fill the remaining seven that constitute a polite chitchat before ditching them for another beer and what you hope will be greener conversational pastures. But you find that the other pastures are equally manure-filled. After an excruciating 111 minutes, you graciously thank the host, making all manner of fabricated excuses about babysitters, likely pet barf, missed dialysis treatments, and so forth to get the hell out of there.

Your Play:

Travel Teams: Do not wait to be asked. The teams looking to pick up players for a travel team are the teams that will be road kill out there on the road.

Find out who is putting together the good team (and this will begin about game *one* of the regular season, not the last game as you might assume). Then lie, cheat and steal to get your kid on it, even if they don't particularly want them.

Parties & Road Trips: Bring a good book (like this one).

Chapter 14: The End of Season Banquet

Indigestion

The perfunctory end-of-year get-together is agony
personified for two reasons:

Bad Potluck

The main course is usually a giant turkey basting pan of
very dry spaghetti that didn't have enough sauce on it
even when it was made back in the 11th century. The
"salad" is nothing but iceberg lettuce in a second turkey
baster. Garlic bread will be there, but never enough that
there is any left by the time the players get through the
line, who by custom get to go first (what is wrong with
this country?). The dessert table is initially impressive
and hopeful with its potpourri of colorful cookies, bars,
and treats. It is also crushingly disappointing as well.
That brownie you select, and are frankly *counting on* to
rescue your evening, will turn out to be a lump of dried
peat moss flavored with oregano.

Boast Masters

But the best is yet to come: The speakers. If you're lucky,
you are just there for a single team, maybe 20 kids, and
so you only have to suffer through about an hour listening
to each coach say something inane and robotic about each
of their players in turn (though oddly, never enough about
your son/daughter, who was the heart and soul of the
team). Unlucky is when it is the CYO Parish Basketball
Banquet consisting of three girls teams and three boys
teams in various age groups. So you're in for like 60

players worth, plus the special recognition awards (for the kid who goes to practice *and* to Mass), the coaching awards, the prayer, the acknowledgements, and so on. If Brevity is the Soul of Wit, then these gatherings seem to apply the maxim Bombastity is the Soul of Shit. It can test a man to his very core.

Your Play:

Okay, so when you're the coach, here are your simple instructions for doing this right:

Food: Put the wife or another highly capable individual in charge of the food with explicit instructions to have it actually taste good. If you have to, collect $20 from every parent and cater it, or just order pizza.

Slide Show: Make sure you or someone else gets pictures of each kid during the year, preferably in a compromised locker room situation, and show them while you talk about each of them.

Funny or Die: Make it funny, make it heartfelt, and make it short. Parents are dying to hear about their kid and don't care a sweaty sock about any other kid. So give them what they want, which is a compliment or observation about the child that you actually considered more than nine seconds before speaking. And make it funny.

Chapter 15: The Board of Directors

Bored Doesn't Begin to Describe It

At some point, you will need to join the Board of one or more of the leagues you're involved with. You will first become aware of the Board's existence because you are enraged by some asinine decision the members have made. After some inquiry, you will be even more enraged because what first appeared to be the good-natured-but rocks-in-their head decision of a pack of golden retrievers may begin to take on the more sinister hallmarks of a pack of weasels. It becomes apparent that decisions tend to go in a direction that is rather advantageous to the Board members and their kids. If you have ever wondered why that one team always seems so stacked even though they are supposed to divide up the talent evenly, it's because the coach and probably a few other parents on that team are on the Board.

Cleaning up Gotham will probably be too hard, so you settle for simple membership within this den of thieves. Problem is, there won't be any vacancies because membership confers a lot of preferential treatment. So you may need to start politicking your ass off to get a seat. Then, get your leather bound notepad out and block off the first Tuesday of the month from 7 pm to 9 pm. Welcome to the Board. You have won a pyrrhic victory.

The end time of 9 PM is, of course, merely suggestive. There is so much to discuss. Each member will opine anywhere from three minutes to three hours on virtually every single issue, no matter how trivial. Should the new flyers be red or blue? 20-minute discussion including segues into paper stock options and the relative copying costs at Kinko's or the secretary's home printer. Should the spring cleanup day be on a Saturday morning or a Sunday morning? 30-minute heated debate involving speculation about potential attendance, personal conflicts of board members, and the relative merits of at least two major religions (this was less of an issue in Minnesota where absolutely everyone is Lutheran anyway). And, speaking of God, may he or she help you if someone tries to make a motion about anything because then it spirals into a veritable orgy of willy-nilly counter motions, amendments, votes to end debate, votes to extend debate, votes on whether we think we're voting on the amendment or the full motion, votes on whether we're allowed a pee break, and votes on whether anyone has any idea of what is going on.

Perhaps the problem is that no one else really listens to us outside of these meetings? Bosses, husbands, wives, children, and pets have all been aggressively tuning us out all day. Now, by virtue of Robert's Rules of Order, someone has to hear you out, especially if you make a motion. So there is some time involved with Board work.

The Lightning Detector Thingamajig
I remember one issue that, all together, swallowed about three or four hours of my life that I will never get back. If I may, I would like to waste about four minutes of your life with it now because in some cosmic sense, I think that helps balance things out. So here goes:

Our humble little baseball organization was loaded. We had been systematically collecting about $75 a kid for years. People paid it without complaint because it was less than the $125 that football costs, the $95 for soccer, or the $750 for hockey. But it didn't cost us that much to run the program. The field use was free. Umps made $35 a game or something. Flyers we printed and posted for registration didn't cost much either. Consequently, we had something like $65,000 in the bank. Nice to have some rainy day money, but it becomes a little uncomfortable for a nonprofit when it comes time to report the swelling bank balance to the IRS. And what can you do? You can discount the next several years of fees to $10, but that kind of freaks people out and all sorts of questions get asked. And then it's really hard to jack it back up again when you need to. Really, besides investing it with Bernie Madoff, all you can do is spend it. But what on? We already had most of the toys: a new batting cage, pitching machine, new bats, etc. The fences were in decent shape. So we had to find something kind of expensive and totally unnecessary to spend the money on. I suggested Segway scooters for all the coaches as a way to help speed up games by letting coaches zip out to the mound for meetings, but that was shot down for some reason. Clearly, the thing that would fall prey to the least objections by any community member who wanted to sniff around our business was something safety related. It's totally defensible.

Consider the following exchange.

Parent: *"You spent $60,000 on what???!"*

Board Member: *"It was for safety."*

Parent: *"Oh. Well, that's fine then."*

Ben Franklin Was Crazy

It is estimated that in a typical year about 85 people die from a lightning strike in the United States. Of those, it's safe to say that probably only about two will be holding baseball bats at the time. And both of them will be in Florida.[9] So that means the odds of it happening to one of our kids was (and I'm being generous here) 2/350,000,000. And that fraction resolved on my HP 12C calculator comes to .00000001; which is just a fancy name for **zero**. And let's not forget that we already had strict safety regulations in place at our ballparks that mandated that if anyone heard thunder anywhere near the ballpark during the previous month, we canceled the season.

So it seemed an abundance of caution. But never mind all that, they sold these really cool, very expensive detectors that could tell you what your senses evidentially cannot: there are some really scary black clouds in the sky, there are huge loud booms thumping your eardrums, and there are bright zig-zaggy flashes lighting up the daytime sky. This machine, somehow, would take those facts in, run some complex calculations, and then sound an alarm if it concluded that there was a lightning storm (presumably a louder sound than the thunder, so you can hear it). Hearing that alarm, we would then know to seek shelter.[10] Just $60,000, or thereabouts. Perfect!

If you are thinking that the four hours of aforementioned lost meeting time was due to debate on the merits of this

---

[9] The rest were golfers, also in Florida.

[10] I believe the same company manufactures a machine that tells you when it is raining outside too. Popular with wicked witches.

purchase, it was not. It was presented to the Board as one of those beyond reproach, fait accompli things (i.e. "The kid's safety is our number one concern!"). Head nods all around. The four hours was just the monthly updates on the safety committee guy's research into these systems, how they work, and how much they cost, and the chairman reiterating how we can't be too careful with the kid's safety, and so on.

In the end, I don't even think we bought the silly thing, though I don't know why. Maybe they got the Segways? I might have dropped dead of boredom by then.

But my son was selected for the all-star team that season, so whatever we bought, it was $60,000 extremely well spent, as far as I was concerned.

Your Play:

Stick to your guns on the Segways.

Chapter 16: Referees

The One-Eyed Man is King

Listen, refs are just guys, or gals, who love the game, want to stay involved, get a little fitness in, and make a little extra scratch on the side. They do their best and get the calls right most of the time, or at least as much as you and I would.

But I still hate their guts. Okay, I admit, I've never done it and would probably make tons of mistakes. But Jesus F---ing Christ, really, that many mistakes? Hard to believe it's possible. I mean what game are they watching? And what's with the attitude? Hell, *"Cheer up, Mr. Zebra! I know you probably go home, make pipe bombs, and dream about blowing up a day care center, but can you leave it at the office?"*

And do not, I repeat, DO NOT, get me started on the Washington State High School Basketball Championship Game in 1981.[11]

Anyway, as I was saying, referees are just doing their job and they don't determine the outcome of games.

---

[11] Go ahead, Google it, but don't get me started.

Chapter 17: Photographs & Video

Boring Your Friends on Facebook

Gear Up

Because you know these moments will be fleeting, and because you are quite literally bursting with pride watching your kid out there, you must capture it all digitally. Shooting sports is, however, a little harder than it looks. So if you're planning to capture this with your point-and-shoot or your iPhone Nimbus 2000, stop right now. Go to Target to pick up more sports gear of some kind and on your way past electronics, pick up a Sony, Canon, or Nikon with the 200mm zoom lens kit. Read the manual if you're the geek type, or do what I do and just start pressing things and clicking things and hope for the best. You will need to take about 4,000 shots for every one that actually looks even close to those you routinely see in newspapers or magazines. And, if you're like me, you somehow won't be able to part with the mediocre ones, so you'll store them all in iPhoto on your iMac and have to continually buy new hard drives to keep up.

Letting the Pros Handle It

There are also still professionals in this game. And they too would like your money.

During your rec league years you will be beholden to the Portrait Guys. These are just like, or sometimes the exact same, as the school photos people. They do low-end weddings on the weekends. They specialize in the time-honored, flat and stodgy, JC Penney-photo style. They also represent a huge pain in your ass, particularly the part of your ass where the wallet sits. The league will set a team pictures date and give you a packet with all of your fantastic photo options: wallet size, 3x5, 8x10, posters, greeting cards, buttons, screensavers, billboards, whatever. You will start to check the box for $7.99 that includes two wallets and a 3x5. Then your wife will grab the pencil and check the box for the "World Series Package" for $59.99 that includes everything listed above and a bonus key chain, because she is convinced that this little group of 8-year-old boys who played seven baseball games together is the stuff of lasting memories that will invite long evenings of scrapbook reminiscing for your child at some point in the future. It turns out that kids are surprisingly unsentimental about any single one of the 2,000 youth teams they will play on in their lives. They won't do much reminiscing and will probably pitch the lot of it by their second move out of college. Nor will you particularly feel like putting on one of the buttons with a profile shot of your son in a baseball cap as you dress for work. But you have one just in case.

Anyway, once the form is filled out and the large check written, you're work is not done. You still have to get your kid into their uniform and make a *special schlep* to the field, rink, diamond, or whatever and wait around while every kid gets a cheesy shot holding a ball, a bat, or a stick, followed by another long wait and then the big team shot. And then you go home, because it's not part of a regularly scheduled game or practice. And you will follow this routine, over and over, four times a year, for about eight years.

There will also be other, more skilled, pros shooting action shots at all the tournaments you attend and eventually at regular high school games. These are actually pretty good photographs. In fact, their shots will be infinitely superior to yours, and you will want them, because your kid looks kind of cool (as opposed to in your shots, where he looks both a little blurry and uncoordinated at the same time). At first you may have a moment of larcenous moral weakening and just think, "Hey, these things are just posted on the web for viewing. I'll just copy and paste and … oh …." Yeah, they sort of have that covered. Unless you don't mind that the shots you send to friends and post on your Facebook page say "Double Play Portraits" emblazoned across the front with a watermark.

Video Killed the Basketball Star
Your fancy camera that I had you buy will also shoot video. Once again, that sounds good. But you will quickly discover that when you watch it later at home, proudly posting it on YouTube for the GPs, it just doesn't quite capture what felt like such a supremely exciting game if you were there. There are two reasons for this. One, your equipment, while hi-def and all of that, still completely sucks compared to what we have all become accustomed to seeing in terms of sports on TV. The other reason is that the game wasn't that exciting to begin with, it only seemed that way to you.

Another curious thing you will discover is that whenever you're filming, your child, or more likely their team, will do something stupid. And the other team will do something brilliant. Then, as you are turning off the camera out of both disgust and to save battery, you will watch as your kid completes the first unassisted (and un-filmed) triple play in your local town's history. This is just the nature of this particular medium.

87

Your Play:

Try, in vain probably, to keep the team photo package purchase to below the $39.99 range. Bank that money for the extravagant Nikon that you want to buy.

Chapter 18: The Empty Dugout

What to Do When It's All Over

That last high school game is a distant memory of a week ago. Your wife has firmly nixed another pregnancy. And a trophy wife just seems like way too much trouble. What now? You're a junkie. You can't just quit. How do you fuel your need for the adrenaline rush of actually giving a rip about a sporting event again? Maybe you are still loyal to your college teams or pro teams? It helps some. You bravely buy a new sweatshirt with the team's logo emblazoned across the chest and print out the schedule. But in comparison to your own flesh and blood, it's feeling a little hollow now. Half the guys on the team are free agent journeymen you don't even recognize from last year. You are rooting for the laundry, as it were. And there is talk about a walkout at the end of the season. Didn't we just do this? Don't remember, don't care.

You try going to a high school game, hoping that somehow the magic will still be there. But all the players are different. You don't recognize any of the parents or the fans. And, *some kid is wearing your son's number — who does he think he is?* They lose, but you don't really feel that bad about it. The passion is gone.

Time to make a clean break. Detox. Rehab. Betty Ford Field.

Your Play:

Here is my 12-step plan (minus nine steps):

Step 1: Drink — This is what we call *transference* in the rehabilitation field. We are essentially transferring one addiction for another.

Step 2: Get a Hobby — It should be something pretty stupid that a drunk can do (obviously, see Step 1) and that has a tendency to create obsessive behavior. Some good candidates include:

- Fishing

- NASCAR

- Folk Dancing

- Ice Fishing

Step 3: Get a Dog[12] — Preferably one of those Frisbee-catching dogs that you can enter into contests. With a little work in the yard, maybe Scout can make it into the regional Canine Flyer Classic this spring and ….

---

[12] Michael Vick, if you are reading this, I retract that statement.

Chapter 19: Just a Game

The score was tied 1 to 1 midway through the 3rd period.
The rink was packed to capacity for a high school hockey
game, the last high school hockey game or competitive
game of any sort my son, a senior and the team captain,
would ever play if they lost. He had been playing hockey
and countless other sports his whole life, with me there
for every second of it from that first day, at age 3, when I
bribed him with the promise of a comic book at the
General Store if he would go out and skate on the town
pond in Norwich, Vt. And it all led up to this moment:
the Vermont State Division 1 Quarter Finals against our
arch rivals. They were better than us. They always had
been. They were a bigger school for one thing, which in
the end almost always provides an advantage in the bell
curve of athletic talent. They were the wealthier school
too, which has its own advantages, and we suffered from
the bitterness of jealousy. They even had the kid who
would that season be named Vermont's "Mr. Hockey,"
who usually scored a pair of goals by himself every
contest. But we had been outplaying them all game and
they were on their heels. We had the emotional edge and
they were playing a little scared. The winner would go on
to the semi-finals, which were played on the big stage, at
the University of Vermont's famed Gutterson Arena, a
place we had never been to during my son's high school
career, in part because the previous year this same team
had beaten us in the quarter-finals. And I wanted that
win, the recognition, the revenge, more than just about
anything I have ever wanted in my life.

A few years ago my brother sent me an email. It had been sent to him in error. He had an email address very similar to another guy somewhere in a Chicago suburb and so he would get this guy's emails occasionally. In it was a rant by one dad to a group of parents about the fact that playing time on their sons' Little League all-star team wasn't fair. It went on for many paragraphs in a semi-hysterical tone about the number of innings their kids had played relative to others and how essentially incompetent and uncaring the coaching staff was. My brother, whose own children were still in the nursery and not yet playing youth sports, sent it to me with that air of dismissive superiority that said, *"Get a load of these nut-job helicopter parents in the Midwest! I mean get a grip (and a life). It's just a game...."*

And I would have agreed with him, at one point in my life. As it was, at that very moment I was *living* that email on two separate Little League teams, one for 10-year-olds, another for 12-year-olds. I had written hundreds of emails (in my head) just like that one to my own sons' coaches as I lay awake at night obsessing about it all. My only response back to my brother was, *"just wait."*

Or consider the story of a recent local Little League team. If you know anything about Little League, you know that it's a tough row to hoe. After forming a town all-star team in June, you have to survive pool play, win your district, win states, and then go on to regionals and finally the Little League World Series in Williamsport, Pa. It's absurdly difficult to do and no team has ever made it past regionals from our state. But this particular team was very good. My older son's team was probably the second-best team in the state that year, and had to face this team in the district finals to determine who would go on to the

92

State tournament. We were just two defensive outs away from the win — and states — when they came roaring back and won, almost as if they knew they would. Then they blew through states and onto regionals in Bristol, Pa., as one of the hottest teams we had sent in years.

Now came a measure of fame and fortune. Every *swing* becomes news in the hometown newspaper. ESPN even *televises* some of the games. I mean if there is anything more exciting than being on ESPN when you are 12 years old, it would have to be seeing your super-hot neighbor and former babysitter sunbathing in the nude by her pool, and that happens even more rarely. Every family member of every kid on that team drops everything in their lives and goes on the road for this; giving bosses the finger, mortgaging homes, and stealing RVs from senior citizens if necessary. Usually, our teams lose three quick games in regional pool play and go home. And it's still totally awesome, just to have been there. But these kids could flat out play, and they were winning. They moved through pool play, elimination rounds, and right into the semi-finals. The winner would play on national TV for the right to go on to the Little League World Series. They played well. They had the other team on the ropes 9 to 8 in the top of the 6th inning and their pitcher was in command. Unfortunately, there was a problem. The coach realized too late that one of his players had still not come up to the plate. The rules say that every player must play three innings in the field and have at least one at bat. The coach, pre-occupied with all the other big and small decisions of the game, had got him in for his three defensive innings, but in a lineup spot that wouldn't get him to the plate until the bottom of the 6th inning. Normally, not a problem. But as the home team, there wasn't going to *be* a bottom 6th if they held the lead. They now found themselves in the very bizarre situation of having to let the other team tie or go ahead in the top of the 6th so that they would have to play the bottom of the 6th and hope to *regain* the lead at that point. The alternative was a forfeit based on a rule violation. So they started intentionally walking hitters and overthrowing bases. The other team, now alerted to what was happening, began swinging at the pitches that were several feet outside the strike zone to deliberately strike out. And so it ended, the points winner going home instead of going on to unprecedented glory for our tiny little state.

It was front-page news all over the state. It was front-page news nationally. It got a huge photo spread in *ESPN* magazine of the players reacting with undisguised agony, tears of frustration and disappointment on the faces of these 12-year-old kids who had worked so hard and come so far. The parents were beside themselves. They felt they had been given this gift, this remarkable blessing that was filling them with pride and excitement. They were going to be shown on national television waving signs with their sons' names and numbers on them. And now, due to a technical coaching error, it wasn't going to happen.

And the coach, well, I don't know. But I think if you asked him, was it *just a game?* he might rip your kidneys out through your eye sockets.

And so there I was, watching that hockey game, heart in my throat. So nervous that I couldn't sit with my wife or anyone I knew. The house was rocking. The whole community was there to see this showdown. With just 10 minutes to play, still knotted at 1 to 1, my son skated toward the boards and delivered the single best check I had ever seen him make. It was beautiful and perfectly legal. And then the ref's arm went up. My son skated to the box in frustration. And then frustration turned to fury and disbelief for him and every one of the fans as the ref signaled a 10-minute major, meaning that we would have to skate with four players for two minutes and then without my son, one of the starting defensemen, for the remainder of the game. But adversity seemed to fuel our team. We killed the penalty and continued pressing for the next eight minutes. With just two minutes to go, the same idiot who whistled Alex called a tripping penalty on our other team captain. It was another horrible call. So for the final two minutes we had to play a man down again. We killed the penalty for 1:52. With eight seconds on the clock and two of our best players still in the box, they had a face-off in our end. Less-experienced players failed to trap the puck in the corner. One of their forwards threw a Hail Mary pass in front of the net, another player slapped at it. It ricocheted off our goalie's skate, off the post and into the net with 1.5 seconds showing. For the second year in a row they (or in this case, the refs) had eliminated us from the state semi-finals and a chance to play at the college rink and on TV. It would have been a dream come true for my son and one that he richly deserved after the countless hours of dedication over the years. And it was gone. I was numb. I couldn't move. It was over and not a thing in the world could bring it back, replay it, fix, or repair it. Despair does not capture my feelings. I will never, ever forget that game.

Was it just a game? Did Bill Buckner just miss a routine grounder? Sweet Jesus, no.

THE END

Appendix

The Armchair Athlete Movie Reviews

No matter how hard you work at taking videos, they're just never going to really be that great. So it's helpful from an inspiration perspective, not to mention an entertainment perspective, to have some professionally produced material in hand.

These are the all-time must-see sports flicks, along with some honorable mention picks. Plus, as a special bonus, those that you want to give a wide berth. Learn from my mistakes here. You're welcome.

Honorable Mention Category

Brian's Song

This is probably a pretty bad film. I think I saw it on TV about 11 times before I was 10 and teared up every single time. But I'm fairly sure that if I tried to watch it now I might be vaguely embarrassed in that Hallmark Special kind of way. But ya gotta love Gale Sayers, right? Anyway, I mention it primarily to date my list. If a film was released before *Brian's Song* I didn't see it, okay? So don't come at me with your *Pride of the Yankees* and all of that.

Bull Durham

Not bad on the first watch. It captures the whole minor league gestalt pretty well. And Tim Robbins' Nuke is worth the ticket. But it doesn't hold up that well. Particularly Kevin's "I Believe" speech, which may have been kind of a man moment back in the '80s but looks pretty effete in the rear view. We were pretty short of man moments, coming off the '70s as we were, era of short shorts, mirrored sunglasses, and Freddy Mercury mustaches. *Bull Durham* seemed pretty bad ass at the time.

Field of Dreams

Is this really a sports movie? Not really, but whatever, Kevin is back. It's worth a watch, once.

Rudy

Ultimate underdog. The film is just okay, but the story is nice.

Jerry Maguire

Love the Cruiser in this, and it's kind of a heart-warmer that is full of quotes that embedded themselves into the culture. It may strain the sports movie definition again. But Tom's former-mentee-turned-cutthroat Bob Sugar, played by Jay Mohr, is priceless.

Quote: "Maguire? Do you think he knows what it's like to be a black guy? —Bob Sugar (who is white)

On the Edge

Bruce Dern stars as a running hermit seeking redemption and justice against the evil Amateur Athletic Association. It may not be your cup of tea if you're not a runner, but it aptly captures the essence of this lonely and honorable pursuit.

Cinderella Man

Russell Crowe is always worth watching. Kind of a *Seabiscuit* in boxing gloves.

Slap Shot

Okay, going for it are the undeniably hilarious Hanson Brothers, who were played with a remarkable degree of restraint when you think about it. Also, it's about hockey. Awesome. So the first 20 minutes of the film are pretty entertaining. The last 1:40 seem like they take about six hours. Very overrated, but still beloved due to the Hanson Brothers, who are to hockey as the Spinal Tap is to rock and roll.

Special Mention Category

Friday Night Lights (TV Series)

While I did not include the film in this list (and it's not bad despite my general discomfort with anything Bill Bob Thornton does; I mean *Sling Blade* notwithstanding, the guy is just kind of creepy) the TV show is freaking awesome. We have been over this.

Top 10 Best Sports Movies ... Ever

#10 *Moneyball*

Makes you the love the business side and believing that you're smarter than all of these ex-jocks who get all the undeserved credit for their feel for the game. Pitt is great (and handsome) as always. Jonah Hill is perfectly cast.

Quote: *"There are rich teams and there are poor teams. Then there's 50 feet of crap. And then there's us." —Billy Beane*

#8 & #9 *Without Limits* & *Prefontaine*

Two decent movies about one completely bad-ass runner from Oregon. It would have been better if they had combined forces and just made one really good movie instead of two so-so ones. But it's not the movies, man, it's the ***man*** … man.

Quote: *"I can endure more pain than anyone you have ever met." —Pre*

#7 *Million Dollar Baby*

Guts and tears. Clint, you are *killing* me. And why do they let that one fighter cheat so bad?

#6 *Chariots of Fire*

Lovely, lyrical, Vangelis, etc. Not super-engaging and not a best picture but will not put you to sleep either, unless you are my wife, who could sleep through an alien attack if it was put in movie form.

Quote (must be spoken in a Scottish accent): *"I know God made me for a purpose, Jenna, but he also made me fast."*

#5 *Rocky*

We love you Rocky. I still run faster on my slogs when the theme song comes on my iPod.

#4 *The Fighter*

Mark Wahlberg is the weakest performance in this thing, and he's fantastic. Christian Bale: I am not worthy.

#3 *Hoosiers*

Perhaps the first modern film of the genre. Gotta love it. No school like the old school.

Quote: *"Coach, I'll make it."* —Jimmy Chitwood

#2 *Remember the Titans*

Denzel, I would follow you to the ends of the earth, or at least watch *RTT* over and over again.

Quote: *"This is no democracy. It is a dictatorship. I am the law."* —Coach Boone

#1 *Miracle*

Okay, it stands on the shoulders of giants. And it's about hockey. Awesome. But if there is a better sports film out there, I will wash my jock with itching powder.
Everything about this thing — from the authentic hockey player actors, the remarkable game situation recreations, and Kurt Russell's absolute channeling of the late, great, legendary Herb Brooks — is perfection. And don't forget, *we beat the fucking Russians!*

Quote:

Craig Patrick: *"Herb, you're missing some of the best players."*

Herb Brooks: *"I'm not looking for the best players, Craig. I'm looking for the right ones."*

Acknowledgements

Many thanks to Joni Cole, Theresa D'Orsi, and Nancy Martin for the great editing. Early draft reads from Jim, Kit, Betsy and Paul B. Inspiration from the Feigs. Marketing from Kit. Thanks to Matt Miller for the help on the cover. Thanks to Chris Charyk for getting me back in the game.

Made in the USA
San Bernardino, CA
27 March 2018